W9-ATR-729

BACKYARD SCIENTIST

BACKYARD BIOLOGY EXPERIMENTS

Alix Wood

PowerKiDS press

New York

Published in 2019 by Rosen Publishing
29 East 21st Street, New York, NY 10010

Produced for Rosen Publishing by Alix Wood Books
Designed by Alix Wood
Editor: Eloise Macgregor
Projects devised and photographed by Kevin Wood

Photo credits:
Cover, 1, 4, 12, 13, 17 bottom, 26, 27 © Adobe Stock Images;
all other photos © Kevin Wood

Cataloging-in-Publication Data
Names: Wood, Alix.
Title: Backyard biology experiments / Alix Wood.
Description: New York : PowerKids Press, 2019. | Series: Backyard scientist | Includes glossary
and index.
Identifiers: LCCN ISBN 9781538337301 (pbk.) | ISBN 9781538337295 (library bound) |
ISBN 9781538337318 (6 pack)
Subjects: LCSH: Biology--Experiments--Juvenile literature.
Classification: LCC QH316.5 W64 2019 | DDC 570.78--dc23

Printed in the United States of America

CPSIA compliance information: Batch # CS18PK: For further information contact Rosen Publishing, New York, New York at 1-800-237-9932.

Contents

What Is Biology?

Biology is the study of living things. "Bio" means life in Greek. Scientists who study biology are called biologists. Biologists examine every kind of life, no matter how big or small it is. They may explore how the human body works, or examine the tiniest **bacteria**. There are lots of jobs that need an understanding of biology. People usually study biology if they want to become a doctor or a vet, for example.

Life Is Everywhere

Look around you now and try to count all the living things you can see. Maybe you can see flowers, trees, and grass. Perhaps you can see a bug, or a bird. If you had a microscope and looked closer, you would be able to see even more living things. On the dinner table, on the floor, in the grass, or even on your skin, there are billions of tiny life-forms!

Setting Up Your Backyard Laboratory

Find an outside space that you can use to do these experiments. Some of them are pretty messy! Remember to check with whomever owns the space that it is OK to do your experiments there. You may want to find a picnic table to work on.

You should be able to find most of the things you will need around your home or yard. You may need to buy some small items, so check the "You Will Need" section before you start a project.

BE SCIENTIFIC

To help study living things, scientists may organize them into different groups, such as "animals" or "plants." This is called **classification**. Things are grouped together depending on how they are the same, and how they are different. Can you sort all living things into sensible groups? It's not that easy. Scientists are still arguing and changing their minds!

STAYING SAFE

Science experiments can be dangerous. The experiments in this book have been specially chosen because they are fun and relatively safe, but you must still be careful. Ask an adult to help you. Follow all warnings. Wear any suggested protective clothing, and be careful.

Grow Some Bacteria

Bacteria are tiny **organisms** that exist all around us. Mostly, bacteria are so small we can only see them using a microscope. Some bacteria can make us sick, so remember to wash your hands after touching dirty surfaces. Try this experiment and find the best conditions for growing bacteria.

YOU WILL NEED:

- heatproof bowl
- two shallow dishes
- cotton swab
- agar powder (in the baking section of food stores)
- plastic wrap
- microwave

1

Stir ½ a teaspoon of agar powder into ¼ cup (60 ml) of hot water in a heatproof bowl. Then **sterilize** it by heating the bowl in a microwave for one minute, making sure it does not boil dry.

2

The agar powder should have completely dissolved and the liquid should be clear. Let the solution cool for a few minutes, then pour a thin layer into both shallow dishes.

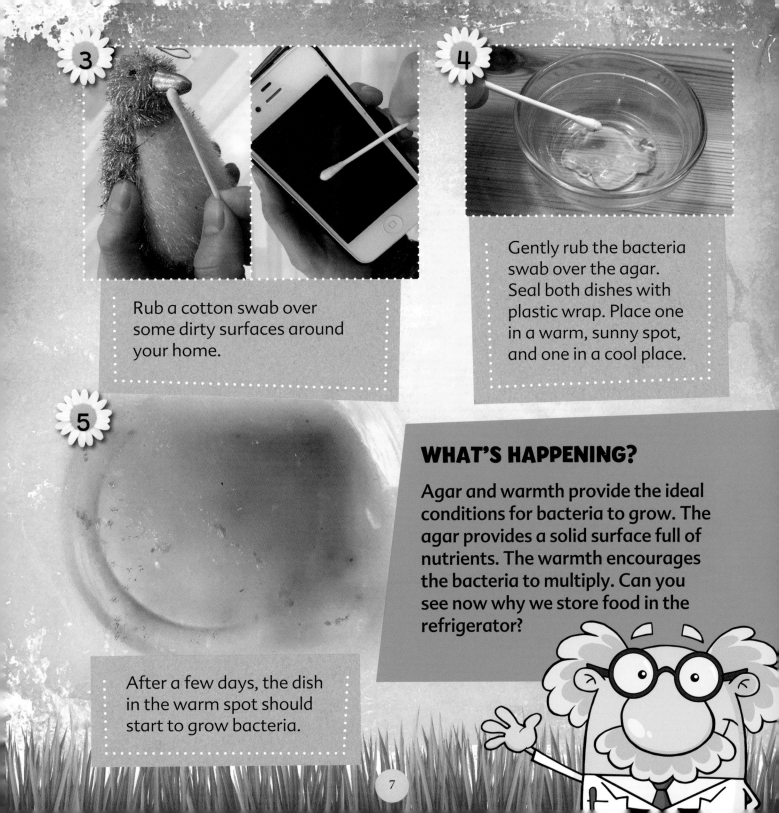

3

Rub a cotton swab over some dirty surfaces around your home.

4

Gently rub the bacteria swab over the agar. Seal both dishes with plastic wrap. Place one in a warm, sunny spot, and one in a cool place.

5

After a few days, the dish in the warm spot should start to grow bacteria.

WHAT'S HAPPENING?

Agar and warmth provide the ideal conditions for bacteria to grow. The agar provides a solid surface full of nutrients. The warmth encourages the bacteria to multiply. Can you see now why we store food in the refrigerator?

Make a Bouncy Egg

Eggs have an outer shell, and an inner **membrane** that protects the **embryo** inside. Usually an egg would break if you dropped it. Try this experiment and make an egg bounce instead. Do this experiment away from pets. They may try to eat the raw egg if it breaks.

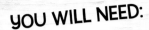

YOU WILL NEED:

- a raw egg
- white vinegar
- a jar
- a kitchen towel
- a ruler

1

Place a raw egg in the jar. Pour in the white vinegar until the egg is completely covered.

2

Bubbles will start to appear on the egg. This is caused by a chemical in the vinegar dissolving a chemical in the eggshell.

3

After 24 hours, take the egg out of the jar. Gently wipe the shell from the egg using a kitchen towel.

4

Your egg should feel rubbery. Now see if it will actually bounce. Find a hard surface. Use a ruler to measure the height you drop your egg from. Start by dropping the egg from a small height. Gradually increase the distance. Did it bounce? At what height did your egg eventually break?

WHAT'S HAPPENING?

Vinegar is a weak acid that reacts with the chemicals that make up the eggshell. The acid starts to break the shell down. This **chemical reaction** produces the bubbles of **carbon dioxide**. The white membrane lining the shell becomes thicker and rubbery.

Keeping Fruit Fresh

Have you ever wondered why an apple starts to turn brown once you cut it? It all has to do with **enzymes**. Enzymes are substances in living organisms that cause a chemical reaction. Enzymes in the apple react to **oxygen** in the air, causing browning. You can slow this down by blocking oxygen from getting on the surface of the fruit. Try this experiment using lemon juice and vitamin C and see which blocks oxygen the best.

YOU WILL NEED:

- two apples
- uncoated vitamin C tablets
- a knife
- a spoon
- a lemon

ADULT HELP NEEDED

1 Ask an adult to help cut two apples and a lemon in half. Keep one half of each apple as a **control**, to compare against your treated halves.

2 Using the back of a spoon, crush two or three vitamin C tablets into a fine powder.

3

Squeeze lemon juice on half of one apple.

4

Sprinkle the powdered tablet on half of the other apple.

5

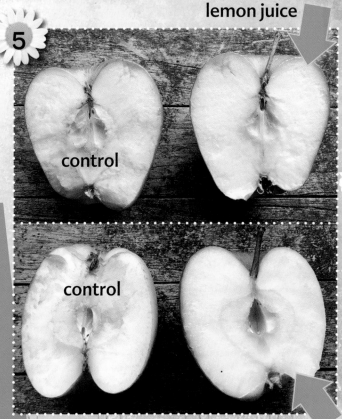

lemon juice

control

control

vitamin C

WHAT'S HAPPENING?

The pictures on the right show the apple halves after one day. The acid in the lemon juice and the **antioxidants** in the vitamin C have both slowed the browning process. Why do you think the vitamin C made the apple look a little orange?

Glowing Beetles

Have you ever seen a glowworm or firefly in your backyard? They can be found in North and South America, Europe, and Asia. If you have some in your neighborhood, try this project and carefully catch and study some fireflies.

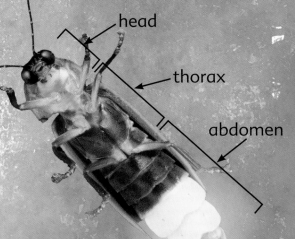

head

thorax

abdomen

WHAT'S HAPPENING?

How do fireflies light up? Enzymes in the firefly cause a chemical reaction inside their bodies. The reaction converts chemical energy into light energy. This type of light production is called **bioluminescence**.

Fireflies glow to attract a mate and to deter **predators**. Each species of firefly flashes their lights in different ways. A female can recognize a light display made by a male of her species!

Fireflies are actually beetles. Like all insects, they have six legs and three body parts: head, thorax, and abdomen. They have tough outer wings, which cover a set of flexible wings used for flying.

First, find your fireflies. They often live around long grass, ponds, marshes, and trees. Get a flashlight and quickly shine it up and down, to mimic a firefly light display.

Fireflies like damp surroundings, so put a moist paper towel at the bottom of your jar. Catch the fireflies carefully using a net. Place them in the jar.

Now you can study these amazing beetles. Different firefly species produce different color glows. The light might be green, yellow, or orange. What color did you find? Let them go as soon as you have finished looking at them, during the same evening. During the day they are more likely to be eaten by predators.

Yeast Power!

Yeast is a living **fungus**. Did you know it is yeast that helps make the holes in a loaf of bread? The yeast makes tiny bubbles in the bread by releasing carbon dioxide gas. To work, yeast needs food, moisture, and warmth. Try this experiment to see how yeast can make enough carbon dioxide to blow up a balloon!

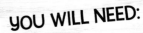

YOU WILL NEED:

- packet of yeast
- small plastic bottle
- 1 teaspoon of sugar
- warm water
- small balloon

1

Wash out the plastic bottle. Pour around 1 inch (3 cm) of warm water into the bottle.

2

Add the packet of yeast. Gently swirl the bottle for a few seconds to mix.

3

Add the sugar and swirl the bottle around again to mix.

4

Blow up the balloon a few times to stretch it. Then stretch the neck of the balloon over the neck of the bottle.

WHAT'S HAPPENING?

The yeast multiplies in the warm, moist environment. The yeast eats the sugar and releases carbon dioxide gas. The gas fills the bottle and then fills the balloon.

5

Leave the bottle in a warm place for around 20 minutes. The balloon should begin to inflate!

Test Your Pulse

When your heart beats, it pushes blood around your body through a network of blood vessels known as **arteries**. As blood is pumped through the arteries it causes a rhythmic throb, or **pulse**. You can tell how fast your heart is pumping by measuring your pulse. Try making this simple tool to check your heart rate.

YOU WILL NEED:

- a marshmallow, or some modeling clay
- a toothpick
- some water
- a timer or stopwatch

1

Wet the bottom of a marshmallow, or roll some modeling clay into a small ball, and flatten the bottom so it is marshmallow-shaped.

2

Press a toothpick halfway into the marshmallow or clay ball. This simple tool is your pulse meter!

3 Rest your arm face up on a table. Place the pulse meter on your wrist, just below your thumb. The toothpick should move with each heartbeat.

4 To find your resting heartbeat, set the timer for ten seconds. Count how many times the toothpick moves. Multiply that number by six to find your beats per minute.

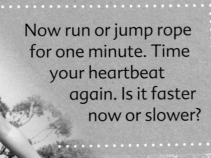

5 Now run or jump rope for one minute. Time your heartbeat again. Is it faster now or slower?

WHAT'S HAPPENING?

Our heart pumps oxygen around our body. It beats somewhere between 60 and 100 times a minute. When we use more energy, our heart beats faster to pump more oxygen around our body.

Make a Working Lung

Lungs supply oxygen to your body. When you breathe in, you inhale oxygen-rich air. Your heart pumps blood to the walls of your lungs to absorb the oxygen and release carbon dioxide. Your lungs then breathe out the carbon dioxide. A membrane at the bottom of your lungs, known as a diaphragm, helps your lungs fill and empty. Make this model to understand how your diaphragm works.

YOU WILL NEED:

- a plastic bottle
- scissors
- a balloon
- a plastic bag
- a rubber band
- some tape

ADULT HELP NEEDED

1 Cut the bottle in half using scissors. You may need an adult to help you.

2 Hold the open end of the balloon and push the rest of the balloon through the neck of the bottle. Stretch the open end around the rim to secure it in place. This is your lung.

3

Cut a square from a plastic bag, large enough to wrap around the base of your bottle. This is your diaphragm. Secure it tightly with a rubber band and tape.

4

Pinch the center of the plastic bag. Push it up and then pull it downward. The balloon inside the bottle will inflate and deflate.

WHAT'S HAPPENING?

As the bag is pulled it creates more space inside the bottle. This causes air to be pulled into the balloon to fill the space. When you push the bag, air from the balloon is pushed out and the balloon deflates. Your lungs' diaphragm works in the same way.

All About Digestion

You can make your own digestive system with this gross experiment. A ziplock bag acts as your stomach, and a pair of panty hose mimics your intestines and bowel. Feed your system some crackers and see what happens as it travels through your homemade digestive tract.

YOU WILL NEED:

- 5 or 6 crackers
- a ziplock bag
- a dish
- vinegar
- water
- scissors
- a panty hose leg or stocking

ADULT HELP NEEDED

1

Break five or six crackers into tiny pieces. This action is mimicking chewing the crackers.

2

Put the cracker pieces into the ziplock bag. Your digestive system is now swallowing the crackers.

3

Add a tablespoon of both water and vinegar. Squeeze the bag, so your hands are acting as the stomach muscles and the vinegar is acting like stomach acid.

4

Pour your stomach contents into a stocking or panty hose leg. Hold over a dish and squeeze any moisture out.

5

Now cut open the foot of the pantyhose leg. Now you can squeeze out your pretend poop into the dish!

WHAT'S HAPPENING?

Digestion allows your body to get nutrients and energy from the food you eat. Your stomach acid breaks down the food. Then, juices in the intestines help digest the food and absorb nutrients. Any leftover waste is turned into poop and leaves the body.

Are You Made of Iron?

Our bodies need a balanced diet to keep healthy. Iron helps our bodies make red blood cells, which carry oxygen around the body. We get iron by eating meat and dark green leafy vegetables. Iron is also added to some foods, such as breakfast cereals. Try this experiment to prove there is real iron in your breakfast cereal. This experiment works best if you use a very strong neodymium magnet.

YOU WILL NEED:

- a cereal with a high iron content
- a blender or mortar and pestle
- measuring cup
- strong magnet
- ziplock bag
- warm water

ADULT HELP NEEDED

IMPORTANT–Magnets are dangerous if swallowed, and can harm electrical equipment. Ask an adult to look after the magnet.

1 Grind up 1 cup of the iron-fortified cereal in a blender, or with a mortar and pestle.

2

Tip the ground cereal into the ziplock bag.

3

Pour a cup of warm water onto the cereal. Seal the bag and leave for a few minutes.

4

Lay the bag flat. Slowly move the magnet in circular movements over the cereal.

5

After several minutes, lift the magnet. You should see a tiny clump of iron. If not, repeat step 4.

WHAT'S HAPPENING?

Iron is digested in the stomach and then absorbed into our bodies in the intestines. If we could collect all the iron from a healthy person's body, there would be enough to make two small nails!

Wrap Up Warm

Our bodies prefer to be at a temperature of 98.6° Fahrenheit (37° Celsius). The clothes we wear help keep us warm. Try this experiment to see which type of fabric is the best **insulator**. Can you predict which fabric would keep us the warmest?

YOU WILL NEED:

- several identical glasses
- some water
- a thermometer
- several different fabrics, such as netting, cotton, linen, and fleece
- pen and paper

1

Get a glass for each fabric you are testing. Add another glass to be your control. It won't be wrapped in a fabric.

2

Fill a jug with warm water. Check the temperature using a thermometer. Add hot or cold water until the thermometer reads 98.6° Fahrenheit (37° C). Then fill the glasses with water.

3

Wrap each glass with a different fabric. Leave the control glass uncovered.

WHAT'S HAPPENING?

Fleece keeps you warm by trapping a layer of warm air around the body, and is a good insulator. Cotton and net are breathable fabrics. They let heat escape to keep you cool on a hot day, so they are not great insulators. Wool is thick and tightly woven, which helps make it a great insulator.

4

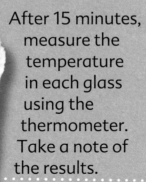

After 15 minutes, measure the temperature in each glass using the thermometer. Take a note of the results.

Choose Right or Left?

Are you left-handed or right-handed? Left-footed or right-footed? Is your right eye **dominant** or is it your left? Try these tests to find out which is your dominant side. Then test a group of friends. See if you can prove if more people are left- or right-dominant.

YOU WILL NEED:

- a pen and paper
- an empty tube
- cup of water
- a small ball
- a soccer ball

1

Test which eye is your dominant eye. Which eye do you wink with? Which eye would you choose to look through an empty tube?

2

Hold up your thumb and line it up with a distant object. Close your right eye. Keep your thumb still and switch eyes. Your thumb will appear to move when you close your dominant eye.

Run forward and jump off one leg. Which did you jump off? Drop a soccer ball on the ground and kick it. Which foot did you use?

Throw a ball. Which arm did you use? What hand would you pick up a cup with? Which hand do you write with?

WHAT'S HAPPENING?

Around 90 percent of people in the world are right-handed. Around 80 percent of people are right-footed and 70 percent have a dominant right eye. Do your results match? Are most people in your study right-dominant?

	Me		Dad		Amy	
Dominant Eye	L	R	L	R	L	R
winking eye		✓		✓		✓
empty tube	✓		✓			✓
lining up thumb	✓			✓		✓
Dominant Foot	L	R	L	R	L	R
Run and jump	✓			✓		✓
Kick a ball		✓		✓		✓
Dominant Hand	L	R	L	R	L	R
throw a ball		✓		✓	✓	
pick up a cup		✓		✓	✓	

Test Your Biology Know-How!

Are you a biology genius? Test yourself with these questions. The answers are on page 29.

1. Biology is the study of living things. What does "bio" mean?
a) study b) life c) things

2. Bacteria grow best in very cold conditions.
a) true b) false

3. What is the protective layer under the shell of an egg called?
a) the embryo b) the membrane c) the yolk

4. You cut an apple in half. Which of the substances below would help keep it from going brown?
a) water b) oxygen c) lemon juice

5. Why do fireflies glow?
a) to attract a mate
b) to keep predators from eating them
c) both of the above

6. What conditions does yeast need to produce carbon dioxide gas?

a) food, moisture, and warmth
b) dry conditions, food, and cold
c) dry conditions, no food, and warmth

7. When we use more energy, our heart beats...

a) faster b) slower

8. What gas do our lungs breathe out?

a) hydrogen b) oxygen c) carbon dioxide

9. Why is some iron good for us?

a) it helps our bodies make red blood cells, which carry oxygen
b) it tastes nice
c) it helps us stand up straight

10. Which of these materials would keep our bodies warmest?

a) lace b) fleece c) cotton

Answers

1. b) life; 2. b) false; 3. b) the membrane; 4. c) lemon juice; 5. c) both of the above; 6. a) food, moisture, and warmth; 7. a) faster; 8. c) carbon dioxide; 9. a) it helps our bodies make red blood cells, which carry oxygen; 10. b) fleece

Glossary

antioxidants A substance that prevents or delays reactions with oxygen.

arteries Tube-shaped vessels that carry blood from the heart.

bacteria Single-celled microorganisms that live in soil, water, the bodies of plants and animals.

bioluminescence The light emitted by organisms such as glowworms and deep-sea fish.

carbon dioxide A heavy colorless gas.

chemical reaction A process in which atoms of the same or different elements rearrange themselves to form a new substance.

classification Systematic arrangement in groups.

control Used as a standard to compare with the results of the other experiment.

dominant Being more effective over others.

embryo An animal in the early stages of development.

enzymes Complex proteins produced by living cells.

fungus Living things that live on dead or decaying organic matter.

insulator A material that is a poor conductor of heat.

membrane A thin, soft, flexible sheet or layer.

organisms Living things.

oxygen An element necessary for life.

predators Animals that kill and eat other animals.

pulse A regular throbbing caused in the arteries by the contractions of the heart.

sterilize To clean something by destroying germs or bacteria.

For More Information

Amson-Bradshaw, Georgia. *Human Body*. London, UK: Wayland, 2018.

Iyer, Rani. *Amazing Life Science Activities*. North Mankato, MN: Capstone Press, 2018.

Parker, Steve. *Bubbling Biology: Fantastic Hands-on Activities*. London, UK: QEB Publishing, 2017.

Thomas, Isabel. *Build Your Own Body*. New York, NY: Bloomsbury Activity Books, 2018.

Websites

Due to the changing nature of Internet links, PowerKids Press has developed an online list of websites related to the subject of this book. This site is updated regularly. Please use this link to access the list:

www.powerkidslinks.com/bs/biology

APR   2019